Blue Line 4

Vokabellernheft

Ausgabe für Bayern (Mittelschulen R-Zug)

Herausgeber: Wolfgang Hamm

Ernst Klett Verlag
Stuttgart • Leipz g

Liebe Schülerin, lieber Schüler,

mit diesem praktischen Vokabellernheft kannst du überall deine Wörter lernen, wiederholen und nachschlagen.

In den Wortlisten zu den Unitabschnitten kannst du Wörter und Wendungen, die dir schwierig vorkommen, mit Textmarker oder Bleistift markieren, um sie dann immer wieder durchzugehen. Außerdem gibt es Schreiblinien, damit du alle Wörter einmal schreiben kannst. So kannst du dir die englischen Wörter besser einprägen.

Die vielen Übungen unterstützen dich bei der Wiederholung der neuen Wörter und Wendungen. Wenn du sie vorher gut gelernt hast, wird dir die Lösung der Aufgaben leichtfallen. So macht dir das Üben sicher Spaß! Hinten im Heft stehen die Lösungen, damit du deine Ergebnisse selbst überprüfen kannst. Außerdem findest du dort eine Liste aller unregelmäßigen Verben, die im Buch vorkommen.

Auf der letzten Seite im Heft befindet sich ein Ben-Lesezeichen. Du kannst es ausschneiden und beim Üben zum Abdecken der linken oder rechten Spalte benutzen.

Viel Erfolg beim Vokabellernen!

Ben's
Blue Line
Bookmark

Let's learn English
together!

Mit Lesezeichen
auf der letzten Seite!

Zoom in – The USA

p. 8	**quiz**	Quiz; Ratespiel	
p. 9	**independence**	Unabhängigkeit	
	flag	Flagge; Fahne	
	dollar ($)	Dollar *(amer. Währungs-einheit)*	

1 Match the words with the definitions.

1. dollar
2. quiz
3. independence
4. flag

a) a symbol of a country
b) when you are free to do what you want
c) lots of questions together
d) there are one hundred cents in one

2 Complete the sentences.

independence   flag   dollar

1. The _____ of the USA is red, blue and white.

2. The USA celebrates its _____ on July 4th.

3. People in the USA use _____ and cents.

Unit 1 Welcome to New York!

Intro

p. 10	**borough**	Stadtteil; Bezirk	
	immigrant	Einwanderer; Einwanderin; Immigrant; Immigrantin	
	statue	Statue	
	island	Insel	
	France	Frankreich	
p. 11	**New Yorker**	New Yorker; New Yorkerin	
	messenger	Kurier; Kurierin; Bote; Botin	
	lake	See	
	multicultural	multikulturell	
	Italy	Italien	
	Italian	italienisch; Italienisch; Italiener; Italienerin	
	population *(no pl)*	Bevölkerung; Einwohner; Einwohnerzahl	

Nimm dir jeden Tag ca. 15 Minuten Zeit,
englische Vokabeln zu lernen.
Am Wochenende wiederholst du dann
alle Vokabeln der ganzen Woche.

1 Find the words and complete the text.

tfboroughvItalypoimmigrantsfimessengersieNewYorkersqsmulticulturallopopulationtitaliant

New York is a very _____ city. There are many _____ who

are part of the _____. Many of these immigrants came from _____,

so there are lots of _____ restaurants in the _____ of Manhattan.

Many _____ are young, and some of them work as bike

_____.

2 Choose the right words to complete the sentences.

1. A _____ (Italian / New Yorker) is someone who lives in New York.

2. A city that people from lots of countries live in is very _____
   (multicultural / population).

3. New York City has five different _____ (immigrants / boroughs).

4. The Statue of Liberty is on a small _____ (lake / island).

5. Central Park in Manhattan is very big and lots of bike _____ (statues /
   messengers) ride through it.

3 Write the words.

1. _____   3. _____

2. _____   4. _____

Topic 1

p. 12	**interviewer**	Interviewer; Interviewerin; Befrager; Befragerin
	Cuba	Kuba
	magazine	Zeitschrift
	for	seit
	home country	Heimat; Heimatland
	decision	Entscheidung
	poor	arm
	opportunity	Chance; Möglichkeit; Gelegenheit
	arrival	Ankömmling
	to **be homesick**	Heimweh haben
	to **get used to (sth)**	sich gewöhnen an (etw.)
	had	past participle von *to have* (haben, essen)
	since	seit; seitdem
	successful	erfolgreich
	career	Laufbahn; Karriere; Beruf
	citizen	Staatsbürger; Staatsbürgerin; Staatsangehöriger; Staatsangehörige
	plan	Plan
	Good luck!	Alles Gute!; Viel Glück!
	future	Zukunft

Das kenne ich schon

going to a new country

immigrant Einwanderer; Einwanderin; Immigrant; Immigrantin

decision Entscheidung

home country Heimat; Heimatland

opportunity Chance; Möglichkeit; Gelegenheit

to **be homesick** Heimweh haben

future Zukunft

to **get used to (sth)** sich gewöhnen an (etw.)

arrival Ankömmling

successful erfolgreich

career Laufbahn; Karriere; Beruf

citizen Staatsbürger; Staatsbürgerin; Staatsangehöriger; Staatsangehörige

to **be a long way away** weit weg sein

different verschieden; unterschiedlich; anders

culture Kultur

country Land; ländliche Gegend

to **miss** vermissen

to **move** umziehen

to **leave** verlassen; weggehen

4 Complete the table.

culture   successful   different   miss   country   leave

career   homesick   move

Verbs	Adjectives	Things

5 Complete the table.

Verb	Simple past	Example sentence
have		She has a good life in the USA.
_____ used to	got used to	He got used to the culture.
_____ homesick	was homesick	I was homesick when I arrived.

6 Complete the text.

Hello! My name is José and I'm from _C_____. I _m_____ to the USA with my

parents and I have lived here _f_____ 13 years. There weren't many _o_____

at home and my family was very _p_____. But now I have been an American

_c_____ _s_____ last year. I can _p_____ my _f_____ –

my parents made the right _d_____ to leave their home _c_____.

7 Match the words with the definitions.

1. interviewer   a) the place where someone is born

2. arrival   b) someone who moves to a different country

3. Good luck!   c) someone who asks questions

4. immigrant   d) you say this when you hope that someone will be successful

5. home country   e) it's like a newspaper

6. magazine   f) when people arrive somewhere

Topic 2

p. 16

nationality	Nationalität; Staatsangehörigkeit	
sign	Schild; Zeichen; Anzeichen	
to **be born**	geboren werden	
parade	Parade; Umzug; Prozession	
apartment *(AE)*	Wohnung; Apartment	
to **walk**	laufen; gehen; zu Fuß gehen	
quick	schnell	
slow	langsam	
Turkish	türkisch; Türkisch; aus der Türkei	
Japanese	japanisch; Japanisch; aus Japan; Japaner; Japanerin	
Spanish	spanisch; Spanisch; aus Spanien	
safe	sicher; ungefährlich; in Sicherheit; unversehrt	
at night	nachts	
zoo	Zoo; Tierpark	

--- Das kenne ich schon ---

city words

apartment *(AE)* Wohnung; Apartment

building Gebäude; Bauwerk

borough Stadtteil; Bezirk

multicultural multikulturell

population *(no pl)* Bevölkerung; Einwohner; Einwohnerzahl

statue Statue

store *(AE)* Laden; Geschäft

traffic Verkehr

capital (city) Hauptstadt

city centre Stadtzentrum; Stadtmitte

noisy laut

park Park

tower Turm

zoo Zoo; Tierpark

8 **Complete the sentences and find the solution for 10.**

1. There are lots of different ___ ⬜ ___ ___ ___ ___ ___ ___ ___ ___ ___ ___ in New York, like Spanish

and Japanese.

2. New York is a very exciting city and there is a big ⬜ ___ ___ ___ ___ ___ every year on Labor Day.

3. When you ___ ⬜ ___ ___ around the city you will see street signs in English and Chinese.

4. Nikolai was ___ ___ ⬜ ___ in Russia, but now he lives in New York.

5. The population is very ___ ___ ___ ⬜ ___ ___ ___ ___ ___ ___ ___ ___ because there are a lot of immigrants.

6. Nikolai ⬜ ___ ___ ___ ___ to New York with his family ten years ago.

7. Life isn't always easy in New York and some parts of the city aren't ___ ___ ___ ⬜ .

8. The city can be very noisy when there are parades, even at ⬜ ___ ___ ___ ___ .

9. There is a lot of traffic in the city ___ ___ ___ ⬜ ___ ___ .

10. Lots of people in cities live in an ⬜⬜⬜⬜⬜⬜⬜⬜⬜⬜ .

9 **Write the words.**

1. _____

2. _____

3. _____

4. _____

10 **Write the opposites.**

1. to be born ⟷ _____

2. slow ⟷ _____

3. dangerous ⟷ _____

4. past ⟷ _____

11 Match the flags with the nationalities.

1.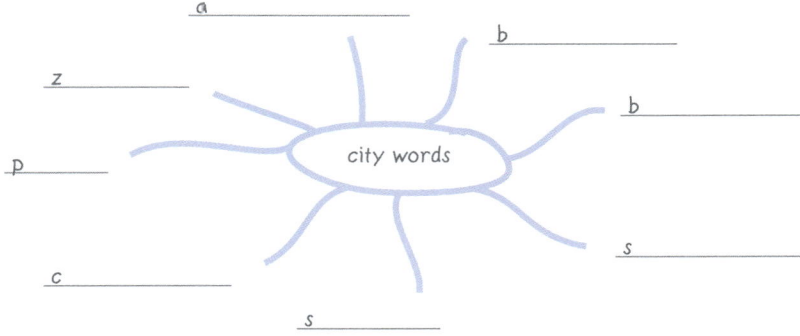

a) Spanish

2.

b) Italian

3.

c) Japanese

4.

d) Turkish

12 Find the wrong word.

1. Spanish • Turkish • Japanese • Cuba

2. immigrant • slow • multicultural • nationality

3. successful • quick • career • opportunity

4. safe • tower • park • zoo

13 Write the city words.

a _____

b _____

z _____

b _____

p _____

city words

s _____

c _____

s _____

Text

p. 20	**witness**	Zeuge; Zeugin
	to **get**	*hier:* holen; bringen
	package	Paket
	to **deliver**	liefern; ausliefern
	van	Lieferwagen; Transporter
	to **knock sb off sth**	jmdn. von etw. stoßen
	to **get out**	aussteigen; herauskommen
	scratch	Kratzer
	to **signal**	*hier:* blinken
	police	Polizei
	knew	simple past von *to know* (wissen, kennen)
p. 21	**wrecked**	demoliert; zerstört; zertrümmert
	driver	Fahrer; Fahrerin
	to **get in**	einsteigen
	to **drive, drove, driven**	fahren; treiben
	to **drive off**	wegfahren
	lady	Frau; Dame
	to **lie**	lügen
	to **prove**	beweisen
	truth	Wahrheit

14 Match the words with the definitions.

1. witness

2. to drive off

3. van

4. knew

5. to get out

6. lady

a) it's like a big car

b) to go away in a car

c) someone who sees an event

d) another word for 'woman'

e) the past tense of 'know'

f) to leave a car

15 Find the words and complete the message.

rigotqewieckedmnpackagedijostfbdriverxatruthikscratchesuydrovelkoffprpolicews

Hi Mom!

Today was an interesting day! I was working as a bike messenger and I was

delivering a _____. A van went past me and knocked me

_____ my bike. There were _____ on the van. My bike

was _____ too! The _____ got out of the van, but

then he _____ back in and _____ off. The _____

came and asked a man some questions. The accident happened outside his flat,

but he didn't tell the _____.

16 Write the words.

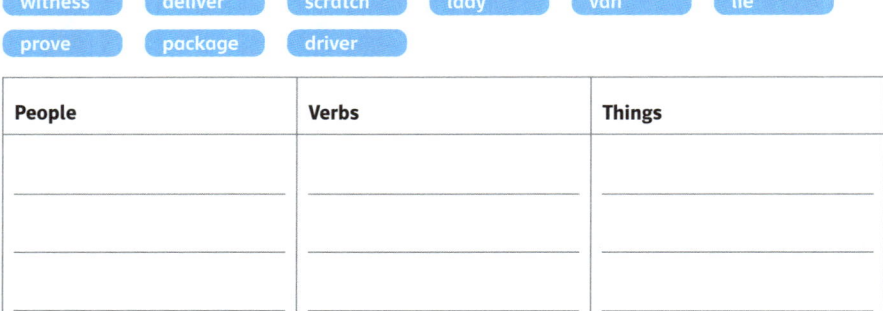

1. _____

3. _____

2. _____

4. _____

17 Complete the table.

witness   deliver   scratch   lady   van   lie

prove   package   driver

People	Verbs	Things
_____	_____	_____
_____	_____	_____
_____	_____	_____

18 Complete the sentences with the verbs.

signal   get   prove   lying   deliver   knocked

1. Bike messengers _____ packages to lots of different people.

2. The messengers have to _____ the packages from different shops.

3. Cars and vans should _____ before they turn right or left.

4. The driver of the van didn't see Alice and he _____ her off her bike.

5. When people don't tell the truth, they are _____ .

6. The police want to _____ that people have done something wrong.

Internet research skills

p. 26

whale	Wal	
whale-watching	Walbeobachtungs-	
to **find out**	herausfinden	
kayaking	Kajakfahren	
kayak	Kajak	
class	Unterricht; Unterrichtsstunde; Kurs	
guide	Führer; Führerin	

19 Choose the right words and complete the sentences.

1. In Cape Cod you can go on a whale-_____ (kayaking / watching) tour.

2. It is fun to go _____ (kayaking / watching) near the beautiful beaches.

3. You can book a _____ (whale / kayak) and use it for one day.

4. You should go online to find _____ (out / in) about Cape Cod.

5. Lots of people take a _____ (witness / class) when they go kayaking.

6. You can book a _____ (lady / guide) who can help you see as many

   _____ (whales / vans) as possible.

20 Write the words.

1.  _____

3.  _____

2.  _____

4.  _____

21 Find the words.

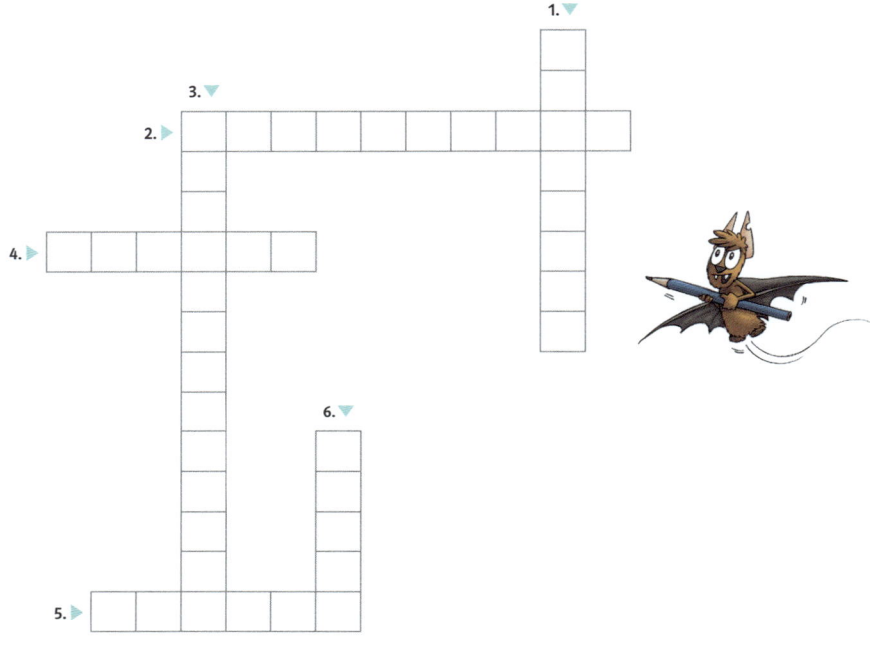

▶

2. Bike … deliver packages.

4. The … of Liberty is a symbol of New York.

5. When there is a problem you can
   call the … .

▼

1. There are five … in New York.

3. New York is very … because there are lots
   of nationalities.

6. A big animal that lives in the sea.

Unit 2 One country – different states

Intro

p. 30	**plane**	Flugzeug
	boat	Boot; Schiff
	wild	wild
p. 31	**surfing**	Surfen; Wellenreiten; Surf-
	landmark	Wahrzeichen
	hill	Berg; Hügel
	cable car	seilgezogene Straßenbahn; Seilbahn
	earthquake	Erdbeben
	of all the states	von allen Staaten
	to **produce**	erzeugen; herstellen; *hier:* anbauen
	vegetable (veg)	Gemüse
	worker	Arbeiter; Arbeiterin; Angestellter; Angestellte
	Hispanic	Hispanoamerikaner; Hispano-amerikanerin; hispanisch
	Mexico	Mexiko

Das kenne ich schon

water transport

boat Boot; Schiff	to **go rafting** raften gehen	**wave** Welle
kayak Kajak	**water** Wasser	**canoeing** Kanufahren
ship Schiff	**river** Fluss	**kayaking** Kajakfahren
raft Raft; Floß	**lake** See	

2

1 Choose the right words and complete the sentences.

1. There are lots of famous _____ (landmarks / states) in California.

2. Lots of tourists go _____ (surfing / canoeing) on the beaches where there

   are very big _____ (waves / vegetables).

3. You can go on famous _____ (wild / cable) cars in San Francisco.

4. Of all the states California _____ (earthquake / produces) the most

   _____ (vegetables / workers).

5. A lot of the workers are _____ (Mexico / Hispanic) and they come from

   countries like _____ (Mexico / Hispanic).

6. You can go to Alaska by _____ (plane / hill) because it is a long way away from

   some roads.

7. There are lots of _____ (wild / boat) animals in Denali National Park which has

   beautiful _____ (cables / rivers) too.

2 **Match the words with the definitions.**

1. earthquake   a) it's like a mountain

2. boat   b) a country that is near the USA

3. plane   c) when the ground moves

4. hill   d) you can go across a sea on this

5. Mexico   e) someone who has a job

6. worker   f) you can fly to another country on this

3 **Complete the table.**

ship   canoeing   river   lake   rafting   kayak

boat   wave   kayaking

Activites	Ways to travel	Water

4 **Write the words.**

1.  _____   3.  _____

2.  _____   4. _____

Topic 1

p. 32	to **look forward to (+ -ing)** — sich freuen auf

himself	sich; selbst; sich selbst
bird	Vogel
grizzly bear	Grizzlybär
wood	Wald
ourselves	uns; selbst; uns selbst
to **sit, sat, sat**	sitzen
myself	mir; mich selbst
to **teach, taught, taught**	lehren; beibringen; unterrichten
themselves	sich selbst
herself	sich selbst; sich; selbst
how to ...	wie man ...
like	als ob
to **enjoy oneself**	Spaß haben; sich amüsieren
yourselves	selbst; euch; euch selbst; sich; Sie sich; Sie sich selbst
if	wenn; falls; ob
yourself	dir; dir selbst; sich; sich selbst
while	während
I'd love (to) ... (= I would love to)	ich würde sehr gern ...; ich hätte gern ...
flight	Flug
airport	Flughafen

> — Das kenne ich schon —
>
> **reflexive pronouns**
>
> **myself** mich; selbst; mir; mich selbst
>
> **yourself** dich; selbst; dir; sich; dir selbst; sich selbst
>
> **himself** sich; selbst; sich selbst
>
> **herself** sich; selbst; sich selbst
>
> **itself** sich; sich selbst
>
> **ourselves** uns; selbst; uns selbst
>
> **yourselves** ihr/euch/Sie/sich (selbst); selbst
>
> **themselves** sich; selbst; sie selbst; sich selbst

5 Find the words and complete the text.

nfsityhbearxctaughtzploveminlookingewhowaqflightibifuxwhilevelikeophimselfytw bzspoow

I'm _____ forward to going to California! My _____ is next month and

I will go to the beach. I _____ myself _____ to surf last year – it's really fun!

It sounds _____ people get very tired _____ they surf but I can just

_____ on the beach _____ I need a break. I'd _____ to go to the _____

in California too – my friend went there last year and he really enjoyed _____.

Maybe I'll see a grizzly _____!

6 Complete the table.

1. I	myself	5. it	_____
2. you	yourself	6. we	_____
3. he	_____	7. you	_____
4. she	_____	8. they	_____

7 Write the words.

1.  _____

2.  _____

3.  _____

4.  _____

Topic 2

p. 36

check-in agent	Check-in-Mitarbeiter; Check-in-Mitarbeiterin
passport	Pass; Reisepass
to **leave**	abfliegen; *hier:* gehen
I'm afraid	leider
delayed	verspätet
about	wegen
to **land**	landen
to **depart**	abfliegen; abfahren
gate	Gate; Flugsteig
boarding time	Einsteigezeit
boarding card	Bordkarte
Have a good flight!	Guten Flug!
another	noch ein; ein anderer; andere
to **complain**	sich beschweren; sich beklagen
suitcase	Koffer
employee	Mitarbeiter; Mitarbeiterin; Arbeitnehmer; Arbeitnehmerin; Angestellter; Angestellte
to **get lost**	verloren gehen; sich verirren
passenger	Passagier; Passagierin

Das kenne ich schon

air travel

airport Flughafen

flight Flug

plane Flugzeug

check-in agent Check-in-Mitarbeiter;
Check-in-Mitarbeiterin

gate Gate; Flugsteig

boarding time Einsteigezeit

suitcase Koffer

passenger Passagier; Passagierin

journey Reise

passport Pass; Reisepass

ticket Ticket

boarding card Bordkarte

delayed verspätet

to **fly** fliegen

to **land** landen

to **depart** abfliegen

to **arrive** ankommen

to **leave** abfliegen; gehen

Have a good flight! Guten Flug!

8 Choose the right verb to complete the sentences.

leave   complain   landed   got   departs

1. You can _____ when there is a problem with your flight.

2. I arrived at the airport in the evening. The plane _____ at 6 p.m.

3. I will _____ my house at 8 a.m. to go to the airport.

4. The plane _____ at 10 a.m. I have to get up early.

5. I'm afraid your suitcase _____ lost when you landed.

9 Match the words with the definitions.

1. delayed

2. suitcase

3. passport

4. check-in agent

5. employee

a) you need this to go to a different country

b) when something happens later

c) another word for 'worker'

d) you pack your clothes in this

e) someone who helps you in an airport

10 Complete the text.

Passenger: Hello. My flight to Los Angeles should l_____ at 10 a.m.

Which g_____ should I go to?

Employee: I'm a_____ your flight is delayed by 30 minutes.

We can't do anything a_____ it. It will d_____ from gate 21.

Have you got your b_____ c_____ ?

Passenger: I think I've lost it.

Employee: That's OK. You can get another one from a check-in a_____ .

_H_____ a g_____ f_____ !

11 Write the air travel words.

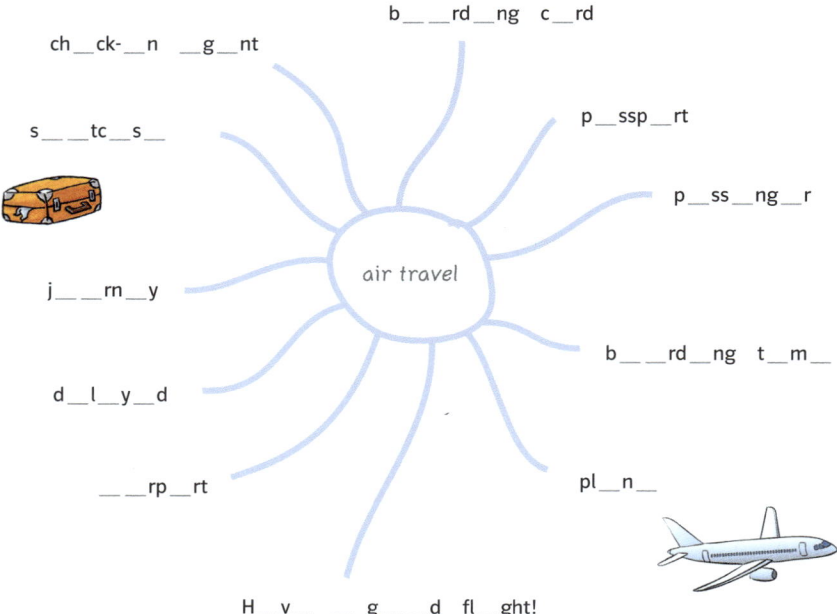

b_ _ _rd_ _ng c_ _rd

ch_ _ck-_ _n _ _g_ _nt

s_ _ _tc_ _s_ _

p_ _ssp_ _rt

p_ _ss_ _ng_ _r

j_ _ _rn_ _y

b_ _ _rd_ _ng t_ _m_ _

d_ _l_ _y_ _d

_ _ _rp_ _rt

pl_ _n_ _

H_ _v_ _ _ _ g_ _ _d fl_ _ght!

Text

p. 40	to **shake, shook, shaken**	beben; zittern; schütteln
	in	bei; an
	to **happen**	vorkommen; sich ereignen
	more often	häufiger; öfter
	to **cause**	verursachen; auslösen
	damage	Schäden; Schaden; Beschädigung
	a year	pro Jahr; im Jahr
	crust	Kruste; Rinde
	plate	Teller; *hier:* (Kontinental-)Platte
	to **move**	(sich) bewegen; ziehen
p. 41	to **destroy**	zerstören
	tsunami	Tsunami *(durch Seebeben ausgelöste Flutwelle)*
	to **design**	konstruieren; entwerfen; gestalten; entwickeln
	during	bei; während
	Richter scale *(no pl)*	Richterskala
	area	Gebiet; Gegend; Areal
	first-aid	Erste-Hilfe-
	item	Ding; Artikel; Gegenstand
	blanket	Decke; Bettdecke; Wolldecke
	can	Dose
	strong	*hier:* stabil

12 Choose the right verbs to complete the sentences.

destroy   cause

happens   design

shakes   moves

1. An earthquake _____ when two plates push against each other very hard

and the earth _____.

2. The ground _____ and this can _____ a lot of damage.

3. Sometimes an earthquake can _____ buildings or bridges.

4. Engineers _____ buildings that are strong so that earthquakes cause less

damage.

13 Find the words and complete the text.

jucansweScaleopDuringxoqblanketseuitemssicrustkdoftenzyyearnktsunamisredamagerr

_____ an earthquake the earth shakes. Earthquakes can happen more

_____ than 500,000 times a _____ and are caused when the earth's

_____ moves. They can cause _____ and lots of _____

if they are high on the Richter _____. People in areas where there are lots of

earthquakes have food in _____, _____ and first-aid

_____.

14 Find the words.

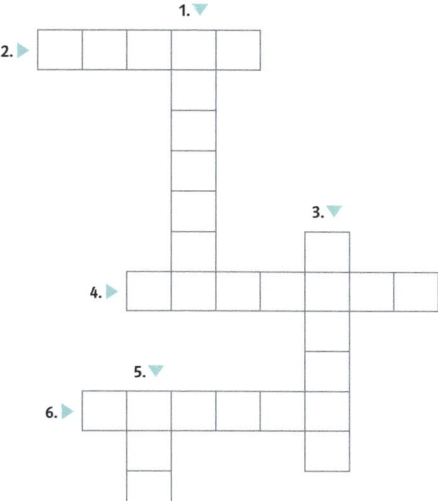

▶

2. A part of the earth's crust.

4. The … Scale shows how strong an earthquake is.

6. Earthquakes … every year.

▼

1. This is like a very big wave.

3. You should sit under a … table in an earthquake.

5. First … can help people who are hurt.

15 Write the simple past.

1. to shake _____

2. to sit _____

3. to happen _____

4. to teach _____

Dictionary skills

p. 48	**sense of smell**	Geruchssinn
	sense	Sinn; Bedeutung
	smell	Geruch; Duft
	to **keep away**	fernhalten
	Alaskan	alaskisch; Alaska-
	husky	Husky (*Schlittenhunderasse*)
	ranger (*AE*)	Ranger; Rangerin
	to **train**	trainieren; eine Ausbildung machen; ausbilden
	sled	Schlitten
	to **transport**	transportieren; befördern
	supplies (*pl*)	Vorräte

— Das kenne ich schon

phrases with -ing

can't stand + -ing etw. nicht ausstehen können; etw. nicht ertragen

to **be good at + -ing** gut sein in; gut sein bei

to **look forward to + -ing** sich freuen auf

to **like + -ing** mögen; gernhaben

to **hate + -ing** hassen; nicht mögen

Lies so oft du kannst englische Texte.
Wie wäre es zum Beispiel mit Nachrichten,
Kurzgeschichten oder Romanen?
Du wirst sehen, dass du auch ohne
Wörterbuch eine Menge verstehst.
Besonders, wenn du dich mit dem Thema
des Textes schon gut auskennst.

16 Complete the sentences.

like   hate   stand   looking forward   good at

sense of smell   Alaskan

1. Grizzly bears have a good _____.

   They're _____ finding food.

2. I want to go to Denali. I _____ climbing _____ mountains.

3. I didn't enjoy myself when I went on the plane to California.

   I can't _____ flying.

4. Are you _____ to going to the national park?

5. I don't want to go to Alaska. I _____ being too cold.

17 Complete the text.

There are some Alaskan _____ (huskies / rangers) in Denali National Park. These

dogs pull _____ (transport / sleds). The _____ (moose / rangers)

in the national park _____ (stand / train) the huskies and the huskies help them

_____ (keep / transport) food and other _____ (senses / supplies).

But they need to keep the supplies _____ (against / away) from the bears because

they have a great sense of _____ (sled / smell).

18 Find the wrong word.

1. husky • smell • grizzly bear • bird   4. myself • during • yourself • itself

2. damage • destroy • tsunami • husky   5. wood • boat • ship • kayak

3. sense • plane • flight • airport   6. landmark • hill • sled • enjoy

— 3 —————————————————————————————————

Unit 3 Southern life

p. 50	**southern**	südlich; Süd-; *hier:* Südstaaten-	

Intro

p. 51	**The Caribbean**	die Karibik	
p. 50	to **get on sth**	in etw. steigen; in etw. einsteigen	
	steamboat	Dampfer; Dampfschiff	
	proud (of)	stolz (auf)	
	African American	Afroamerikaner; Afroamerikanerin	
p. 51	to **enjoy**	genießen; Gefallen finden an	
	climate	Klima	
	Barbados	Barbados *(Inselstaat in der Karibik)*	
	tourist industry	Tourismus	

Lerne Vokabeln zusammen mit Freunden. So könnt ihr euch gegenseitig abfragen und helfen. Vielleicht habt ihr sogar Tipps, die die/der andere noch nicht kennt?

1 Complete the text.

> steamboat   enjoy   Caribbean   tourist   African   climate
> area   southern   on   proud

The _____ industry is very important in the _____ states. For example,

lots of people get _____ a _____ on the Mississippi River near New

Orleans. The _____ is also very multicultural and lots of _____ Americans

live there. The _____ also has a strong culture and the people are very

_____ of it. If you _____ going to the beach, you will love Barbados –

it has a great _____!

2 Match the words with the definitions.

1. to enjoy   a) a lot of islands to the south of the USA

2. Barbados   b) what the weather is like somewhere

3. climate   c) from the south of the USA

4. the Caribbean   d) to like doing something

5. southern   e) an island in the Caribbean

Topic 1

p. 52	**Thanksgiving**	Erntedankfest
	holiday *(AE)*	Feiertag
	son	Sohn
	to **be able to (do sth)**	(etw. tun) können; (zu etw.) fähig sein *(Ersatzform für can)*
	a few	ein paar; einige; wenige
	Take a seat.	Setz dich.; Setzen Sie sich.; Nimm Platz.; Nehmen Sie Platz.
	turkey	Truthahn; Pute
	meat	Fleisch
	annoyed	verärgert
	I don't mind.	Es macht nichts.
	corn	Mais; Korn; Getreide
	potato *(sg)*, **potatoes** *(pl)*	Kartoffel
	thankful	dankbar
	happy	froh; fröhlich
	to **be allowed to (do sth)**	(etw. tun) dürfen

— Das kenne ich schon —

food and drink

meal Mahlzeit; Essen

meat Fleisch

turkey Truthahn; Pute

chicken Hähnchen; Huhn

burger Hamburger

hot dog Hotdog

fish *(sg)*, **fish** *(pl)* Fisch

vegetable (veg) Gemüse

salad Salat

corn Mais; Korn; Getreide

potato *(sg)*, **potatoes** *(pl)* Kartoffel

chips *(pl)* Pommes frites

rice Reis

fruit Obst; Frucht

strawberry Erdbeere

plum Pflaume

apple Apfel

banana Banane

pizza Pizza

sandwich Sandwich; belegtes Brot

butter Butter

drink Getränk

tea Tee

3 Complete the dialogue.

Janet: Take a _s_____ everybody. It's great to see everyone for

      _T_____ . It's my favorite _h_____ .

Sherrie: Thank you for inviting us! I'm very _t_____ .

      It's good to see your _s_____ again.

Janet: I know that you're a vegetarian, so you're not _a_____ to eat _m_____ .

      I cooked lots of _v_____ , but we will eat _t_____ too.

Sherrie: This is a great _m_____ ! Am I _a_____ to have some

      _c_____ and a _f_____ _p_____ ?

Janet: Of course! I don't _m_____ .

      _H_____ Thanksgiving everybody!

4 Write the synonyms.

1. I am able to   _____

2. It's not important to me.   _____

3. some   _____

4. Sit down.   _____

5 Write the words.

1. _____

2. _____

3. _____

4. _____

6 Complete the table.

| pizza | turkey | plum | strawberry | sandwich | chicken |

| fish | salad | banana |

Meals	Fruits	Meats

7 Write the food and drink words.

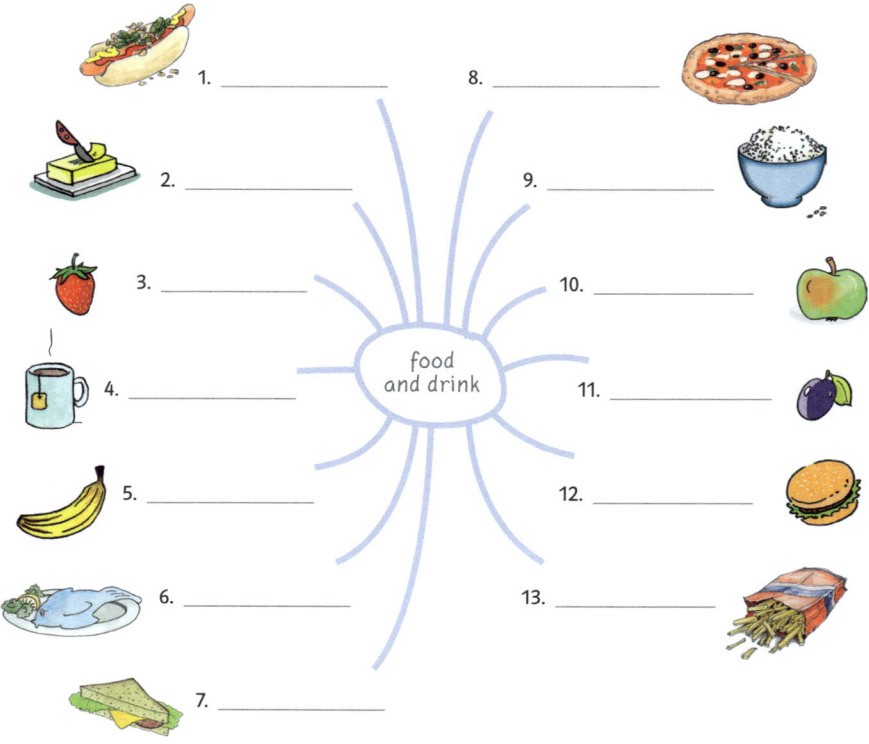

1. _____

2. _____

3. _____

4. _____

5. _____

6. _____

7. _____

food and drink

8. _____

9. _____

10. _____

11. _____

12. _____

13. _____

Topic 2

p. 56	**Caribbean**	Karibe; Karibin; karibisch	
	gun	Pistole; Schusswaffe; Waffe	
	nurse	Krankenpfleger; Krankenschwester	
	hotel	Hotel	
	to **disagree**	anderer Meinung sein; nicht einverstanden sein	
	violence *(no pl)*	Gewalt	
	drug	Droge	
	to **rely (on)**	sich verlassen (auf); vertrauen (auf)	
	forever	für immer; ewig	
	comment	Kommentar	
	to **avoid**	aus dem Weg gehen; vermeiden; meiden; ausweichen	
	vet	Tierarzt; Tierärztin	
	assistant	Helfer; Helferin; Assistent; Assistentin; Mitarbeiter; Mitarbeiterin	
	to	für	
	hairdresser	Friseur; Friseurin	
	hairdressing salon	Friseursalon	
	manager	Manager; Managerin; Geschäftsführer; Geschäftsführerin	

--- Das kenne ich schon ---

phrasal verbs

to **ask about** fragen nach; sich erkundigen nach

to **drive off** wegfahren

to **fall off** von etw. stürzen; herunterfallen; hinunterfallen

to **find out** herausfinden

to **get in** einsteigen

to **get out** aussteigen; herauskommen

to **get up** aufstehen

to **sit down** sich setzen; sich hinsetzen

to **take out** hinausbringen

to **talk to** reden mit; sprechen mit

8 Complete the sentences and find the solution for 8.

1. I want to ☐_ _ _ out about the culture of the Caribbean.

2. Some people think that Jamaica is a dangerous place because there is a lot of

   _ _☐_ _ _ _ _ .

3. Other people _ _ _ _ _☐_ _ because they think that the islands are very beautiful.

4. The tourist industry is very important in the Caribbean, and Aman's brother is going to be a

   hotel _ _ _ _ _☐_ .

5. Some people in Jamaica move to the USA because they want to _☐_ _ _ the problems

   in the Caribbean.

6. Aman wants to live in Jamaica and work as a hairdresser in

   a _ _ _ _ _ _☐_ _ _ _ _ salon.

7. Family is very important to lots of Caribbean people and they ☐_ _ _ on their parents.

8. I will be interested in the Caribbean ☐☐☐☐☐☐☐☐ .

9 Complete the table.

| rely | violence | drugs | manager | hairdresser | disagree |
| guns | avoid | nurse |

Jobs	Verbs	Problems

10 Find the words and complete the text.

violencedCaribbeannhvetdecommentixassistantgaoutwdrugsjhotelrforeverhrtos

Jamaica is in the _____. I work as an _____ at

a _____ but I don't want to live here _____.

In the future I want to go to the US and be a _____ – I will find _____

about another culture! Life can be difficult because there are a lot of

_____ and _____. But the country is important

_____ me. I want to know what you think. Write a _____!

11 Complete the sentences.

out   about   down   in   off   to   up

off   on   out   out

1. The man got _____ the car and drove _____.

2. She sat _____ on the steamboat and then she fell _____ her seat.

3. I want to find _____ what life in Jamaica is like. I will talk _____ Tara about it.

4. My family is very important to me. I rely _____ them.

5. I'm looking forward to going to Barbados. I asked my brother _____ it.

6. I went to bed very late last night, so I got _____ at 11 a.m. today.

7. I saw my friend when she got _____ of the van.

8. My mum is going to take the meat _____ of the meal because my brother is a vegetarian.

Text

p. 60	**century**	Jahrhundert	
	to **hear about**	erfahren von; hören von	
	to **keep sb prisoner**	jmdn. gefangen halten	
	to **escape**	entkommen; fliehen; entfliehen; flüchten	
	dead	tot	
	so that	damit; sodass	
	canoe	Kanu	
	sky	Himmel	
	probably	wahrscheinlich	
	boom	Donner; Boom	
	smoke	Rauch	
	to **shoot, shot, shot**	schießen; erschießen	
	body	Leiche; Körper	
	to **go fishing**	angeln gehen; fischen gehen	
	Miss	Frau *(Anrede)*	
	slave	Sklave; Sklavin	
p. 61	**ghost**	Geist; Gespenst	
	after	nachdem	
	anyone	irgendjemand; irgendeiner	
	slave trader	Sklavenhändler; Menschenhändler	
	swam	simple past von *to swim* (schwimmen)	
	to **explore**	erkunden; erforschen	
	cave	Höhle	

Das kenne ich schon

conjunctions

so that damit; sodass	**before** bevor; vorher; zuvor	**if** wenn; falls; ob
after nachdem	**because** weil; da	**when** als; wenn
while während	**so** also; deshalb	

12 Complete the text.

Have you __h_____ about The Adventures of Huckleberry Finn? The story happens in the

19th __c_____ and Huckleberry Finn __e_____ after his dad __k_____

him prisoner. People think that he is __p_____ dead and Huckleberry hears a

__b_____ when they try to find his __b_____. When he is on an island he meets Jim,

__M_____ Watson's __s_____, who thinks that Huckleberry is a __g_____.

__A_____ Huckleberry tells him what has happened they find a __c_____.

They __e_____ the cave __w_____ they are on the island.

13 Complete the sentences.

while · after · before · because · when · so · so that · if

1. A steamboat full of people went down the river _____ people can find Huckleberry Finn.

2. The people do not know _____ Huckleberry is dead or not _____ they didn't find him.

3. Huckleberry saw the boat _____ he went fishing, _____ he knew he was safe.

4. Huckleberry saw Jim _____ he walked through the woods.

5. Jim thought that Huckleberry was a ghost _____ he saw him.

6. Huckleberry and Jim found a cave _____ they were exploring the island.

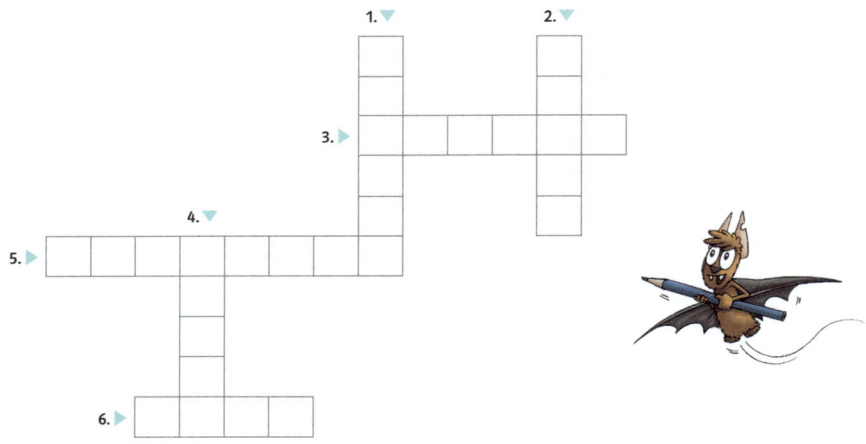

14 Write the words.

1.  _____

2.  _____

3.  _____

4.  _____

15 Find the words.

1.▼ 2.▼

3.▶

4.▼

5.▶

6.▶

▶

3. Miss Watson didn't want to sell Jim to … worse than her.

5. If you are kept … you will want to escape.

6. When someones dies they are … .

▼

1. A slave … wanted to buy Jim.

2. It's like a kayak.

4. This is caused by fire.

16 Write the simple past.

1. swim _____

2. go fishing _____

3. keep prisoner _____

4. escape _____

Vocabulary skills

p. 66 | **hurricane** | Hurrikan; Orkan; Wirbelsturm | |
interview	Interview; Gespräch; Befragung	
movement	Bewegung	
impossible	unmöglich	
given	past participle von *to give* (geben, schenken)	
to **rebuild**	wiederaufbauen	

> **Das kenne ich schon**
>
> **climate**
>
> | **climate** Klima | **wind** Wind | **dry** trocken |
> | **hurricane** Hurrikan; Orkan; Wirbelsturm | **cold** Kälte | **hot** heiß |
> | | | **cold** kalt |

17 Write the words that belong to the same word family.

1. move _____

2. possible _____

3. interviewer _____

4. build _____

18 Match the words with the definitions.

1. cold

2. wind

3. dry

4. hurricane

5. climate

6. hot

a) when there is lots of wind and rain

b) the opposite of cold

c) there is snow when the weather is like this

d) another word for the weather

e) a movement in the air

f) when there is no water

19 Find the words.

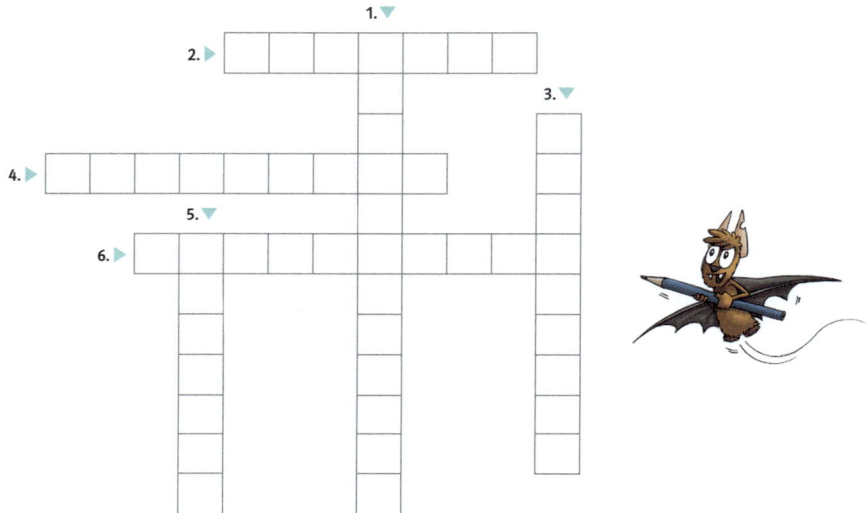

2. A hundred years.

4. There are a lot of African ... in the southern states.

6. When you can't do something it is ...

1. This is a holiday in the USA.

3. When someone asks somebody questions.

5. Another word for 'boss'.

Unit 4 Working in Canada

Intro

p. 70	**ice hockey**	Eishockey
	second	zweit-
	border	Grenze
p. 71	**wilderness**	Wildnis
	moose *(sg)*, **moose** *(pl)*	Elch
	both	beide
	colony	Kolonie
	French	französisch; Französisch; aus Frankreich
	language	Sprache
	Canadian	Kanadier; Kanadierin; kanadisch; aus Kanada
	Inuit	Inuit *(Ureinwohner Kanadas)*
	group	Gruppe

Bestimmt hast du englische Lieblingslieder oder -raps. Aber verstehst du auch, worum es darin geht? Druck dir doch mal einen Text aus dem Internet aus und versuche, ihn sinngemäß zu übersetzen und auswendig zu lernen. Dabei lernst du viele neue Wörter, die du sicher auch super behalten kannst.

1 **Complete the text.**

Canada is the __s_____ largest country in the world and is very multicultural.

For example, in Quebec people speak __b_____ English and __F_____ .

The Inuit are a __g_____ of people in the north of Canada and they also have a different

__l_____ . They live in the __w_____ where you can see __m_____

and other animals. But most people in Canada live near the US __b_____ .

2 **Match the words with the definitions.**

1. Canadian   a) people who live in the north of Canada

2. colony   b) where two countries meet

3. Inuit   c) someone who lives in Canada

4. ice hockey   d) an area which is part of another country

5. border   e) a sport which is popular in Canada

Topic 1

p. 72	**fair**	fair; gerecht	
	update	aktuelle Information; Update; Aktualisierung	
	app	App	
	TV	Fernseh-; Fernsehen	
	series *(no pl)*	Serie	
	to **mean, meant, meant**	meinen; bedeuten	
	selfie	Selfie	
	software	Software	
	copyright	Copyright; Urheberrecht	
	follower	Follower; Followerin; Anhänger; Anhängerin	
	to **comment (on)**	kommentieren	
	tutorial	Tutorial; Anleitung	
	to **repair**	reparieren	
	episode	Folge; Episode	

3 Match the words with the definitions.

1. TV

2. to repair

3. to comment

4. series

5. app

a) to write a message on a post online

b) a lot of episodes together

c) another way of saying 'television'

d) you have this on your phone

e) to make something better again

4 Complete the dialogue.

Josh

Hey Megan! 😊 I saw your _s_____

on my social media _a_____ – it looks good!

Megan

Thanks! One of my _f_____ has

_c_____ on the photo. Have you seen

the new TV _s_____ yet? I've watched two

_e_____ today.

Josh

No, I'm watching a _t_____ now.

It tells me how to find songs that don't have

_c_____ on them.

Megan

Cool! I have to go now and help Dad cook dinner –

it's not _f_____ !

Josh

I know what you _m_____ !

5 Choose the right words and complete the sentences.

1. I can get _____ (software / updates) about sports on an _____

   (app / series).

2. I've bought some new _____ (follower / software).

   I'm going to watch a _____ (tutorial / comment) to find out how to use it.

3. Some people watch lots of _____ (selfies / episodes) in one day on

   their _____ (TV / copyright).

4. I need to _____ (repair / comment) the TV, it doesn't work anymore.

Topic 2

p. 76	**application**	Bewerbung
	receptionist	Empfangschef; Empfangsdame
	guest	Gast
	to **look for**	suchen (nach)
	experience	Erfahrung; Erlebnis
	customer service	Kundenbetreuung; Kundendienst; Kundenservice
	skill	Kenntnis; Fertigkeit; Fähigkeit; Geschick
	to **offer**	bieten; anbieten
	salary	Gehalt
	training	Ausbildung; Training
	CV (curriculum vitae)	Lebenslauf
	letter of application	Bewerbungsschreiben
	letter	Schreiben; Brief; Buchstabe
	Dear ...,	Sehr geehrte(r) ...,
	to **apply (for)**	sich bewerben (für/um)
	internship	Praktikum; Berufspraktikum
	travel agent's	Reisebüro
	confident	selbstsicher; selbstbewusst; sicher
	reliable	verlässlich; zuverlässig; vertrauenswürdig
	Yours sincerely,	Mit freundlichen Grüßen

6 Match the words that go together and write them down.

1. letter of
2. travel
3. customer
4. Yours
5. ice

a) hockey
b) sincerely
c) application
d) service
e) agent's

_____
_____
_____
_____
_____

7 Find the words and complete the letter.

internshipDearCVYoursexperiencetrainingreliableletterconfidentapplytravelskilloffer

_____ Mrs Walker,

I am writing to _____ for the job at your _____

agent's. I am a _____ worker and I am very _____.

I can _____ a lot of _____ and I have also done

an _____ as a receptionist at a travel agent's so I have

_____ of the job. I would love to do some

_____ to find out more about the job.

I am sending you my _____ with this _____.

I look forward to hearing from you.

_____ sincerely,

Martin Henderson

8 Find the words.

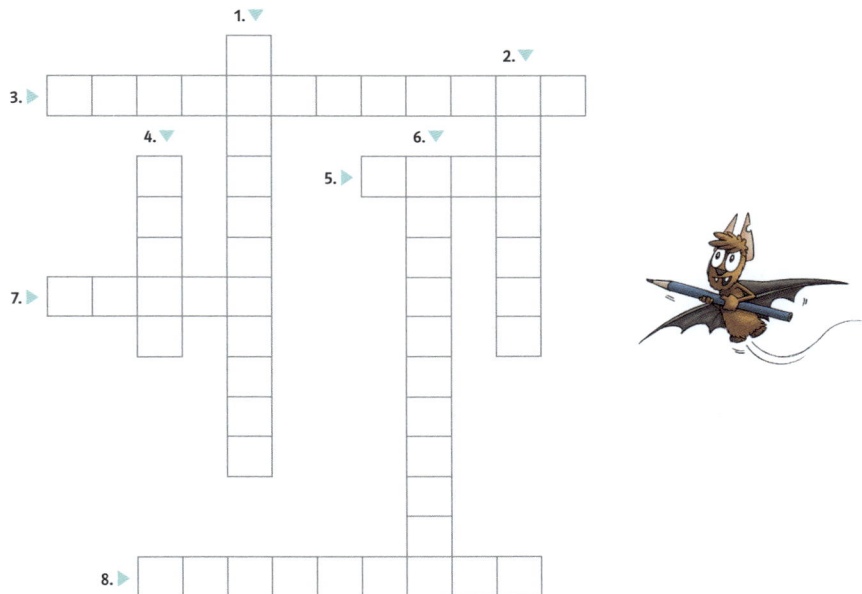

3. Someone who works in a hotel.

5. You start a letter with this.

7. Someone who goes to a hotel.

8. You end a letter with 'Yours …'.

1. You can write a letter of …

2. It is important to have good customer … for some jobs.

4. You hope the company can … you a job.

6. If you do an internship you will get good work … .

Text

p. 80	**railway station**	Bahnhof
	railway	Eisenbahn; Bahn
	flexible	flexibel
	working hours *(pl)*	Arbeitszeit
	hours *(pl)*	Zeiten
	secondary school leaving certificate	mittlerer Schulabschluss; Realschulabschluss
	friendly	freundlich; sympathisch
	travel agent	Reisebürokaufmann; Reisebürokauffrau
	to **plan**	planen
	to **make reservations**	reservieren
	qualification	Ausbildung; Qualifikation; Abschluss; Schulabschluss
	tourism	Tourismus
	efficient	effizient; leistungsfähig
p. 81	**address**	Adresse
	date of birth	Geburtsdatum
	education	Ausbildung; Erziehung; Bildung
	secondary school	weiterführende Schule; Mittelschule
	primary school	Grundschule
	Russian	Russisch; russisch; aus Russland; Russe; Russin
	interest	Interesse
	reference	Referenz; Arbeitszeugnis; Empfehlung
	available	erhältlich; verfügbar
	request	Anfrage

─ Das kenne ich schon ─

travel words

tourism Tourismus

travel agent Reisebürokaufmann; Reisebürokauffrau

travel agent's Reisebüro

guide Führer; Führerin

bed and breakfast (B & B) Frühstückspension

hotel Hotel

to **travel** reisen

to **transport** transportieren; befördern

railway station Bahnhof

to **get on sth** in etw. steigen; in etw. einsteigen

to **get off** aussteigen

cable car seilgezogene Straßenbahn; Seilbahn

to **drive off** wegfahren

driver Fahrer; Fahrerin

─ Das kenne ich schon ─

words for talking about jobs

education Ausbildung; Erziehung; Bildung

experience Erfahrung

training Ausbildung; Training

career Laufbahn; Karriere; Beruf

working hours *(pl)* Arbeitszeit

salary Gehalt

to **offer** bieten; anbieten

to **train** eine Ausbildung machen; ausbilden

successful erfolgreich

efficient effizient; leistungsfähig

confident selbstsicher; selbstbewusst; sicher

reliable verlässlich; zuverlässig; vertrauenswürdig

friendly freundlich; sympathisch

9 Match the words with the definitions.

1. Russian

2. flexible

3. railway station

4. salary

5. interest

6. travel agent

a) you are given this when you have a job

b) something that you like doing

c) when something can be changed

d) somebody who comes from Russia

e) somebody who helps people to book a holiday

f) you can get on a train from here

10 Complete the table.

plan   railway   available   friendly   apply   offer

qualification   successful   hotel   get on   experience   efficient

Verbs	Adjectives	Things

11 Complete the travel words.

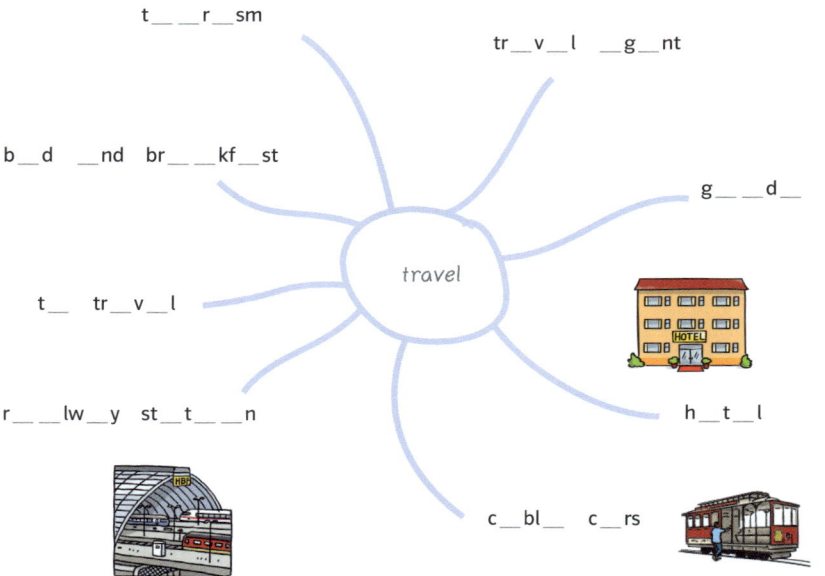

t__ __r__sm

tr__v__l   __g__nt

b__d   __nd   br__ __kf__st

g__ __d__

t__   tr__v__l

r__ __lw__y   st__t__ __n

h__t__l

c__bl__   c__rs

12 Choose the right words and complete the sentences.

1. When you write your CV you should give your _____ (address / business) and

   _____ (school / date) of birth.

2. You should give your secondary and _____ (working / primary) schools under

   'Education'.

3. You should have a _____ (request / qualification) in

   _____ (interest / tourism) if you want to be a travel agent.

4. The company will want to see a secondary school leaving _____ (hours /

   certificate) and they could make a _____ (railway / request) for references.

5. A travel agent _____ (plans / makes) reservations and

   has _____ (flexible / available) working _____ (hours / schools).

13 Complete the table.

hotel   cable car   salary   driver   career   training

bed and breakfast   efficient

Travel	Jobs

Speaking skills

p. 88 **topic**   Thema

kilometre (km)   Kilometer (km)

14 Match the words with the definitions.

1. kilometre   a) where you live

2. address   b) a part of a TV series

3. topic   c) one thousand metres

4. episode   d) something you talk about

15 Find the wrong word.

1. rely • enjoy • canoe • shoot

2. friendly • confident • tourism • reliable

3. software • app • selfie • CV

4. hot • hours • cold • dry

5. request • receptionist • guide • travel agent

6. hotel • travel • railway station • update

16 Complete the table.

Verb	Simple past	Example sentence
mean	_____	Do you know what I mean?
get on	_____	You can get on the train now.
_____	applied	I applied for the job.

17 What are the words?

a) Find the words.

E	H	I	L	L	P	Y	G	M	H	Z
B	O	G	Q	G	L	Q	B	O	D	B
S	C	R	B	U	A	V	V	O	I	L
W	Y	S	U	I	T	C	A	S	E	A
L	U	M	I	E	E	A	O	E	O	N
R	A	O	Y	H	X	N	P	R	Y	K
N	S	K	D	V	C	P	L	A	N	E
S	L	E	D	D	B	O	A	T	Q	T

b) Write them down.

▶ ▼

 1. _____

 6. _____

 2. _____

 7. _____

 3. _____

 8. _____

 4. _____

 9. _____

 5. _____

 10. _____

Hier findest du alle unregelmäßigen Verben, die im Buch vorkommen. Die Liste enthält jeweils alle drei Formen, auch wenn sie noch nicht in den Units vorgekommen sind.

infinitive	simple past	past participle	German
to **be**	**was, were**	**been**	sein
to **become**	**became**	**become**	werden
to **bring**	**brought**	**brought**	(mit)bringen
to **build**	**built**	**built**	bauen
to **buy**	**bought**	**bought**	kaufen
to **catch**	**caught**	**caught**	fangen; nehmen
to **choose**	**chose**	**chosen**	wählen; auswählen
to **come**	**came**	**come**	kommen
to **cost**	**cost**	**cost**	kosten
to **do**	**did**	**done**	machen; tun
to **drink**	**drank**	**drunk**	trinken
to **drive**	**drove**	**driven**	fahren; treiben
to **eat**	**ate**	**eaten**	essen
to **fall**	**fell**	**fallen**	fallen
to **feed**	**fed**	**fed**	füttern
to **feel**	**felt**	**felt**	(sich) (an)fühlen
to **fight**	**fought**	**fought**	kämpfen; (sich) streiten
to **find**	**found**	**found**	finden
to **fly**	**flew**	**flown**	fliegen
to **forget**	**forgot**	**forgotten**	vergessen
to **get**	**got**	**got**	bekommen; werden; kommen; holen; bringen
to **give**	**gave**	**given**	geben; schenken
to **go**	**went**	**gone**	gehen; fahren
to **have**	**had**	**had**	haben; besitzen

infinitive	simple past	past participle	German
to **hit**	hit	hit	schlagen; treffen
to **hold**	held	held	(fest)halten
to **hurt**	hurt	hurt	verletzen; wehtun
to **keep**	kept	kept	(be)halten
to **know**	knew	known	kennen; wissen
to **leave**	left	left	(ver)lassen; abfahren; weg-gehen; vergessen; hinterlassen
to **lose**	lost	lost	verlieren
to **make**	made	made	machen; tun; bilden
to **mean**	meant	meant	bedeuten; meinen
to **meet**	met	met	(sich) treffen
to **put**	put	put	setzen; legen; stellen
to **read**	read	read	lesen; vorlesen
to **ride**	rode	ridden	fahren; reiten
to **ring**	rang	rung	klingeln
to **run**	ran	run	laufen; rennen
to **say**	said	said	sagen; sprechen; nennen; nachsprechen
to **see**	saw	seen	sehen
to **sell**	sold	sold	verkaufen
to **send**	sent	sent	schicken; senden
to **shake**	shook	shaken	beben; zittern; schütteln
to **shoot**	shot	shot	(er)schießen
to **show**	showed	shown	zeigen
to **sing**	sang	sung	singen
to **sit**	sat	sat	(sich) (hin)setzen; sitzen
to **sleep**	slept	slept	schlafen
to **speak**	spoke	spoken	sprechen
to **spend**	spent	spent	verbringen; ausgeben
to **stand**	stood	stood	stehen; ertragen; aussteheri

infinitive	simple past	past participle	German
to **swim**	**swam**	**swum**	schwimmen
to **swing**	**swung**	**swung**	schwingen; schwenken
to **take**	**took**	**taken**	nehmen; (hin)bringen; dauern; brauchen
to **teach**	**taught**	**taught**	lehren; beibringen; unterrichten
to **tell**	**told**	**told**	erzählen; sagen
to **think**	**thought**	**thought**	denken; glauben
to **throw**	**threw**	**thrown**	werfen
to **understand**	**understood**	**understood**	verstehen
to **wake up**	**woke up**	**woken up**	aufwachen; erwachen; aufwecken
to **wear**	**wore**	**worn**	anhaben; tragen
to **win**	**won**	**won**	gewinnen
to **write**	**wrote**	**written**	schreiben

Zoom in

1 1.d; 2.c; 3.b; 4.a
2 1. flag; 2. independence; 3. dollars

Unit 1

Intro

1 multicultural, immigrants, population, Italy, Italian, borough, New Yorkers, messengers
2 1. New Yorker; 2. multicultural; 3. boroughs; 4. island; 5. messengers
3 1. island; 2. lake; 3. France; 4. statue

Topic 1

4 Verbs: miss, leave, move; Adjectives: successful, different, homesick;
Things: culture, country career
5 had, get, be
6 Cuba, moved, for, opportunities, poor, citizen, since, plan, future, decision, country
7 1.c; 2.f; 3.d; 4.b; 5.a; 6.e

Topic 2

8 1. nationalities; 2. parade; 3. walk; 4. born; 5. multicultural; 6. moved; 7. safe; 8. night;
9. centre; 10. apartment
9 1. apartment; 2. parace; 3. tower; 4. zoo
10 1. to die; 2. quick; 3. safe; 4. future
11 1.c; 2.d; 3.a; 4.b
12 1. Cuba; 2. slow; 3. quick; 4. safe
13 apartment, building, borough, statue, store, capital, park, zoo

Text

14 1.c; 2.b; 3.a; 4.e; 5.f; 6.d
15 package, off, scratches, wrecked, driver, got, drove, police, truth
16 1. to signal; 2. van; 3. package; 4. scratch
17 People: witness, lady, driver; Verbs: deliver, lie, prove; Things: scratch, van, package
18 1. deliver; 2. get; 3. signal; 4. knocked; 5. lying; 6. prove

Internet research skills

19 1. watching; 2. kayaking; 3. kayak; 4. out; 5. class; 6. guide, whales
20 1. kayak; 2. whale; 3. park; 4. sign
21 ▶ 2. messengers; 4 Statue; 5. police
▼ 1. boroughs; 3. multicultural; 6. whale

Unit 2

Intro

1 1. landmarks; 2. surfing, waves; 3. cable; 4. produces, vegetables; 5. Hispanic, Mexico; 6. plane;
   7. wild, rivers

2 1.c; 2.d; 3.f; 4.a; 5.b; 6.e

3 Activities: canoeing, rafting, kayaking; Ways to travel: ship, kayak, boat; Water: river, lake, wave

4 1. raft; 2. ship; 3. river; 4. wave

Topic 1

5 looking, flight, taught, how, like, while, sit, if, love, woods, himself, bear

6 3. himself; 4. herself; 5. itself; 6. ourselves; 7. yourselves; 8. themselves

7 1. grizzly bear; 2. airport; 3. wood; 4. bird

Topic 2

8 1. complain; 2. landed; 3. leave; 4. departs; 5. got

9 1.b; 2.d; 3.a; 4.e; 5.c

10 leave, gate, afraid, about, depart, boarding card, another, agent, Have a good flight!

11 check-in agent, boarding card, passport, passenger, boarding time, plane, Have a good flight!,
    airport, delayed, journey, suitcase

Text

12 1. happens, moves; 2. shakes, cause; 3. destroy; 4. design

13 During, often, year, crust, tsunamis, damage, Scale, cans, blankets, items

14 ▶ 2. plate; 4. Richter; 6. happen
    ▼ 1. tsunami; 3. strong; 5. aid

15 1. shook; 2. sat; 3. happened; 4. taught

Dictionary skills

16 1. sense of smell, good at; 2. like, Alaskan; 3. stand; 4. looking forward; 5. hate

17 huskies, sleds, rangers, train, transport, supplies, away, smell

18 1. smell; 2. complain; 3. sense; 4. during; 5. wood; 6. enjoy

Unit 3

Intro

1 tourist, southern, on, steamboat, area / Caribbean, African, Caribbean / area, proud, enjoy, climate

2 1. d; 2. e; 3. b; 4. a; 5. c

Topic 1

3 seat, Thanksgiving, holiday, thankful, son, able, meat, vegetables, turkey, meal, allowed, corn, few, potatoes, mind, Happy

4 1. I can; 2. I don't mind; 3. a few; 4. Take a seat.

5 1. turkey; 2. salad; 3. corn; 4. potato

6 Meals: pizza, sandwich, salad; Fruits: plum, strawberry, banana; Meats: turkey, chicken, fish

7 1. hot dog; 2. butter; 3. strawberry; 4. tea; 5. banana; 6. fish; 7. sandwich; 8. pizza; 9. rice; 10. apple; 11. plum; 12. burger; 13. chips

Topic 2

8 1. find; 2. violence; 3. disagree; 4. manager; 5. avoid; 6. hairdressing; 7. rely; 8. forever

9 Jobs: manager, hairdresser, nurse; Verbs: rely, disagree, avoid; Problems: violence, drugs, guns

10 Caribbean, assistant, hotel, forever, vet, out, drugs, violence, to, comment

11 1. in, off; 2. down, off; 3. out, to; 4. on; 5. about; 6. up; 7. out; 8. out

Text

12 heard, century, escapes, kept, probably, boom, body, Miss, slave, ghost, After, cave, explore, while

13 1. so that; 2. if, because; 3. before, so; 4. after; 5. when; 6. while

14 1. canoe; 2. ghost; 3. sky; 4. cave

15 ▶ 3. anyone; 5. prisoner; 6. dead
    ▼ 1. trader; 2. canoe; 4. smoke

16 1. swam; 2. went fishing; 3. kept prisoner; 4. escaped

Vocabulary skills

17 1. movement; 2. impossible; 3. interview; 4. rebuild

18 1. c; 2. e; 3. f; 4. a; 5. d; 6. b

19 ▶ 2. century; 4. Americans; 6. impossible
    ▼ 1. Thanksgiving; 3. interview; 5. manager

Unit 4

Intro

1 second, both, French, group, language, wilderness, moose, border

2 1.c; 2.d; 3.a; 4.e; 5.b

Topic 1

3 1.c; 2.e; 3.a; 4.b; 5.d

4 selfie, app, followers, commented, series, episodes, tutorial, copyright, fair, mean

5 1. updates, app; 2. software, tutorial; 3. episodes, TV; 4. repair

Topic 2

6 1.c; 2.e; 3.d; 4.b; 5.a

7 Dear, apply, travel, confident, reliable, offer, skills, internship, experience, training, CV, letter, Yours

8 ▶ 3. receptionist; 5. Dear; 7. guest; 8. sincerely
▼ 1. application; 2. service; 4. offer; 6. experience

Text

9 1.d; 2.c; 3.f; 4.a; 5.b; 6.e

10 Verbs: plan, apply, offer, get on; Adjectives: available, friendly, successful, efficient; Things: railway, qualification, hotel, experience

11 tourism, travel agent, guide, hotel, cable cars, railway station, to travel, bed and breakfast

12 1. address, date; 2. primary, Education; 3. qualification, tourism; 4. certificate, request; 5. makes, flexible, hours

13 Travel: hotel, cable car, driver, bed and breakfast; Jobs: salary, career, training, efficient

Speaking skills

14 1.c; 2.a; 3.d; 4.b

15 1. canoe; 2. tourism; 3. CV; 4. hours; 5. request; 6. update

16 meant, got on, apply

17 1. hill; 2. suitcase; 3. plane; 4. sled; 5. boat; 6. plate; 7. moose; 8. blanket; 9. smoke; 10. can

Ben's Blue Line **Bookmark**

Let's learn English together!

Ben's
Blue Line
Bookmark

Let's learn English together!